As If Faith Can Be Somehow Learned

poems by

Daryl J. Lukas

Finishing Line Press
Georgetown, Kentucky

As If Faith
Can Be Somehow Learned

Copyright © 2020 by Daryl J. Lukas
ISBN 978-1-64662-136-1 First Edition
All rights reserved under International and Pan-American Copyright Conventions. No part of this book may be reproduced in any manner whatsoever without written permission from the publisher, except in the case of brief quotations embodied in critical articles and reviews.

Publisher: Leah Maines

Editor: Christen Kincaid

Cover Art: Daryl J. Lukas

Author Photo: Diane Lukas

Cover Design: Elizabeth Maines McCleavy

Printed in the USA on acid-free paper.
Order online: www.finishinglinepress.com
also available on amazon.com

Author inquiries and mail orders:
Finishing Line Press
P. O. Box 1626
Georgetown, Kentucky 40324
U. S. A.

Table of Contents

The Disciple 1

A Morning Prayer 2

Directions to Muirfield 3

The Vestige 4

The Battle of Fallen Timbers 5

While Shopping at Costco 6

Something Genuine 7

Summer Wind 8

Mrs. Kwapich 9

A Rare Find 10

Colors 11

Irene 12

Gray 13

Talking About Golf 14

Two Guys Talking at the Four Horsemen Tavern 15

Walking Past the Jeep Plant 16

Rules of Engagement 17

Nine Miles to Trenton 18

Tiger Stadium 20

Moon River 21

About You 22

The Stud Finder 23

What I Did Today 24

Put-In-Bay, Ohio 25

Parkersburg 26

Dempsey vs. Willard 27

When I Came Back Dying 28

Serendipity 29

A Parallel Universe 30

Monday Morning 31

Victoria 33

Reunion 34

Across the Street from the Funeral Home 35

The Last Laugh 36

Artistic License 38

Van Gogh 39

Advice from a Sinner 41

How It Begins 42

Having Never Been to Idaho 44

The Writer 45

Charlie the Dog 46

Making Love 47

Apocalypse 48

Myrtle Beach 49

The Other Man 51

Petoskey 52

Hope 54

Faith 56

The Grotto 58

Delaney 59

The Polish Cavalry 60

Bright Lights 62

January 63

Heaven 64

Acknowledgments 65

Bio 67

for Diane

The Disciple

As my wife backs her Jeep
down the drive, on her way to Chicago,
and our dog Charlie and I wave good-bye
from the front porch, with his drooping tail
and with a look of great concern
in his caramel-colored eyes,

I suddenly realize that I have become my grandmother,
reminding her to "drive safe" and to "call me"
when she gets there.

And for the next several hours
I'll pace inside the house saying Hail Marys
while talking to myself or to Charlie,

and say *o Jezu*, (yah-zoo)
which is "oh Jesus" in Polish,
whenever I hear a clap of thunder
or sirens in the distance, or especially

if the phone does indeed ring,

when I can almost hear the creaking of her rocker,
going back and forth in that tiny dining room,
and see my *busia* (boo-sha) clutching her rosary

before getting up and walking into the kitchen,
with her poor old knuckles
turning white.

A Morning Prayer

After finishing my glass of tomato juice,
lightly seasoned with pepper and one raw egg,

I went to the screen door and gazed outside
at the beauty that I try to never overlook, or take
for granted, when living in the state of Michigan
and knowing that the summers don't really
last forever,

with the sunshine and blue skies, and with that
perfect breeze upon my skin, being only
a temporary condition.

So, that's why I make it a special point, *each day*,
to stand there and observe the plum tree,
with its deep red leaves,

and the cumulus clouds
when they're as white as cotton,

and the irises and daisies, and the succulents
and ferns, and the marigolds and wildflowers
while each is in full bloom.

But today, out of the corner of my eye, I noticed my wife
as she was watering the garden, with her light blonde hair
blowing so gracefully in the wind

and I saw our dog, sprawled in the grass, with his paws
in the air like a dead armadillo.

Then I whispered,

*Thank you for this day, oh Lord,
and for the many blessings that have been
bestowed upon me,*

Amen.

Directions to Muirfield

Drive north through Ohio
to State Line Road, turn left
and go another mile or so,
we're beyond that grove of Sycamore trees,
just around the first bend.

You'll see a DEAD END sign
with bold, black letters,
then simply follow those boot prints
through the snow,
or you can trace that scent
of smoke in the air
back to a pile of burning branches.

And there'll be a museum of bottle caps, mostly beer,
scattered amongst the sticks and brown leaves,
and this curious collection of wind-blown paper
from seemingly every far corner
of the world.

Or you can watch the Canada geese
as they fly toward the northeast
and listen . . .

it's where they'll honk a "good-morning" to that couple
waving below,

from their secluded acre of mortgaged earth
on this street
with a Scottish name.

The Vestige

There was a time in America, unlike today,
when there were people who actually knew the meaning of the word
haberdashery, and when men wore hats.

But, unfortunately, along with the names like "Fedora" and "Panama"
and good ol' "Derby," for the most part, they've disappeared.

Of course, there are some men who wear cowboy hats
or baseball caps, but it's not the same; and even so, like an idiot,
I threw my favorite cap away—the one I purchased at a bar
in Petoskey, Michigan, at a place called "Papa Lou's"
and had worn almost every day for the past five years
with the beguiling words *bordello and billiards*
sewn into the soft, gray fabric.

And I'd be wearing it now
if my wife hadn't threatened me with divorce—well,
not exactly, but almost.

"It stinks," she said. So I washed it.

Then she said, "It still stinks."

(And, to her credit, there may have been a slight odor.)

However, maybe women just can't understand
a man's need to hold onto something to the point
of disintegration—if it feels right.

Like a pair of blue jeans, or a flannel shirt.

Or a marriage.

Or underwear.

The Battle of Fallen Timbers

On a division of highway in Northwest Ohio,
better known to the locals as the Anthony Wayne Trail,
a sign reads,

"Exit 67—Fallen Timbers Battlefield and Monument,"

and while driving by the other day
I began to recall those times from my youth
when I had wondered,

*what kind of person would actually pull-off the highway
and spend the day in that peculiar section of woods
along the Maumee River*

where, in 1794, what's been called the "last battle
of the American Revolution" took place

and General "Mad Anthony" Wayne, after being summoned
out of retirement by President George Washington, defeated
a confederacy of Native American tribes

led by such dignitaries as Chief Blue Jacket of the Shawnee,
Chief Little Turtle of the Miami, and Chief Turkey Foot
of the Ottawa, among others.

But then, on that raw and blustery February morning,
I found that I was the one going another mile down Route 24
and turning right,

and I was that lone soul retracing the steps
of the thousands of heroic men who fought there,
the infantry and light infantry, the regulars and volunteers,
the Dragoons and Kentucky marksmen, and even those brave
musicians, on that hallowed ground where so many lost their lives

and through which a tornado had passed a few years earlier
to provide the battle with its famous name—that, on one cold day
in 2018, was almost forgotten.

While Shopping at Costco

It was a Friday morning in June,
with the parking lot already three-quarters full by 10,
and even though that gigantic warehouse was built
for the explicit purpose of buying and selling in bulk,
with hundreds of pallets and thousands of enormous boxes,
my wife had sent me there for only one thing—garbage bags.

However, upon entering that modern-day kingdom, without the aid
of a compass, or a map, or, at the very least, a dependable horse,
and with no idea of where this treasure might be found,
I kept wandering around in circles like Don Quixote
until I met this chivalrous young attendant named "Brad."

"Excuse me," I said, "I'm sorry to bother you, but
I'm looking for garbage bags."

And, with a puzzled look on his face, as if to suggest
that I had come from a different time and was speaking in some
ancient dialect, he replied, "Garbage bags?"

Then, after pausing for a moment, he asked,

"Do you mean—*trash* bags?"

I gave him a blank stare.

"Yeah," I answered slowly, looking him straight in the eyes,
"I guess that I mean—*trash* bags."

"That would be aisle thirty-six . . . no, wait a minute, make that
thirty-eight," he said, "all the way at the back of the store."

Then he pointed.

"Ok," I said, "thanks."

So, with the sun at my back, presumably, and with lawn furniture
and display tables yet to slay, I headed west.

Something Genuine

We noticed each other
from across the street
as I was walking by,
a moment of indecision.
She was water-soaked, maybe four,
wearing a purple bathing suit
while adorning the sprinkler on her front lawn.

We shared an instant of self-consciousness,
I don't have a place to hide,
then she un-crisscrossed her hands
that were covering her knobby little knees
and gave the most unpretentious smile.

Then we smiled at each other
and waved good-bye
as she went running back through the spray,
and I continued along
feeling ebullient in spirit,
thankful for having received
such a gift.

Summer Wind

There are better things in life I'm sure
than to be sitting in a bar on a weekday afternoon
with the sunlight softly filtering through the half-drawn shades
and feeling the subtle breeze as it continues to gently blow
from one open door to the other;

and listening to the traffic and to the jukebox play Sinatra
while leaning back and drinking another beer,
and smelling that aroma of fajitas in the air
as it comes drifting from a restaurant
down the street;

and staring at a photograph that's hanging on the wall
of a legendary football player named Bronko Nagurski,
as if it were a painting left inside a Spanish cave
of antelope and bison and deer;

and as the rest of the world goes on spinning outside
with people doing whatever it is
that they do,

wondering about what could've happened
to the saber-toothed tigers and woolly-mammoths
while remembering the greatest fullback
that ever lived.

Yes, there are better things in life to be sure,
but not many.

Mrs. Kwapich

Her name was pronounced "Kwa-pik,"
or "kwa-Peesh," if from the old country,
this heavyset woman with a thick Polish accent
who lived in our neighborhood
when I was a kid.

Mostly I remember her sweeping,
her front stoop and sidewalk,
and the fact that she never knew
my first name—or the names of my brothers.

Yet, each fall, when the ground was covered with red and orange,
and with some yellow and purple and brown—and even blue,
she would call to me from her backyard,

"Hey! You there! Lukas boy! You come rake leaves, yah?
I give you quarter."

And I would pretend not to hear.

However, sometime later, my father would invariably find out
and in his most foreboding tone he'd say,

"Go rake her leaves right now, young man—and if she offers you
a quarter say, *No thank you*."

And so, I did.

A Rare Find

Last night, as we were walking along the beach,
my wife found a plastic cup that she filled
with sea shells.

Some big, some small, though most were about the size
of a half-dollar. She brought them back to our hotel room,
washed the sand off, and laid them out to dry.

Then she studied them in intimate detail, with some no bigger
than a spec, or flea, and with their intricate beauty hidden
from everyone but her.

She looked at them in the same way
that she used to peruse tiny diamonds in necklaces and rings
when she worked for a jewelry store,
back when we first met,
years ago.

And before that I had often wondered
what kind of woman would ever marry the likes
of me.

Colors

I love their names.

Red. Yellow. Blue.

So simple. So perfect.

I love seeing their names on the side of a crayon.

Orange. Green. Purple.

I love seeing them arranged in a brand new box of 64
and how they complement one another.

I love seeing them in my wife's garden or on billiard balls
as they go rolling across a felt-covered table. And, perhaps
especially, how vibrant they remain after coming to rest.

When random. When in a state of happenstance.

As they were that morning in my father's basement
so many years ago, after his buddies had left at two
but with their cigar smoke still hanging in the room.

I loved those colors. I loved that smell.

And as I sat on the steps, next to the bar and pool table,
I thought how each ball was simply a varying degree
of the others—like the color wheel at school.

How perfect!

I love how life is like an unfinished game.

Irene

She sits waiting on her barstool with cigarette in hand
and peers out into the night at what used to be
her city, now strangers to one another.

She sits waiting in the darkness, in the shadow of her youth
for the suitor who never comes, who never magically appears
through the wispy clouds of her freshly-puffed Pall-Mall
though lurking around every corner of time and place,
so she waits.

She sits waiting like her city, once so cavalier,
and speaks of downtown and the Tiedtke's Building,
of Swayne Field and the Mud Hens, of Willys-Overland
and the Jeep, of cherry blossoms in the spring
and her mother's backyard; she speaks of anything
to anybody willing to listen, while she sits

waiting,
waiting,
waiting,

for the sealed envelope,
for the loved one's ear,
for the kiss good-bye.

Gray

When I was ten, lying on the living room floor
watching our old TV, I found it hard to believe
that he was actually letting *Ilsa* walk away.
Yet, with each excruciating step through that moonlit fog,
as if some arbitrary measure between right and wrong,
their distance grew—until finally, she was gone.

And years later, as his pistol was pointing straight at the heart
of *Major Strasser*, with a stony-faced determination
that as a young man I had always admired, I realized
that I was now older than Bogart had been and wondered
how that was possible.

And last night, while sitting in front of my giant flat screen,
I found it rather hard to believe that I was once more
following that winding trail on that marvelous map,
through Europe and Africa, to a place called *Casablanca*,
just so I could see the world again
in black and white.

Talking About Golf

for Jerry Lukas (1930-2002)

I would try to visit my parents every week, for Sunday
dinners. It was a chance to converse with my mom
about son and mother things, and to talk to my father
about baseball or football, whichever was in season,
and furnaces and tomatoes and automobiles. But mostly, we would talk
about golf. Oh, how he loved that game.

Even in the dead of winter, he'd be as excited as a schoolboy
when showing me the latest addition to his collection of clubs
he kept in the basement where we would practice our swings,
so effortlessly—before he was diagnosed with cancer.

But several years have now passed since the day
my father called me on the phone:
"I can't golf anymore," he said,
"I can't make the swing,"
while deep down inside I was actually praying
of course you can, you're my father, you can do anything
as I began foolishly retelling a story
that he had first relayed to me about a wayward
professional golfer (at the time I couldn't remember his name)
who, after seeking his father's advice, had once again found
his game—by slowing everything down. "His name was
Bert Yancey," my father said, "But you don't understand,"
then he told me how he had lost his balance during a swing
while attempting to play one last round with his friends.
I tried to sound encouraging but, looking back,
he had called to tell me that he was dying—and when he said,
"Keep your eye on the ball" and "Remember to hit 'em straight,"
I think I now know what he was really saying.

And when I next visit his grave, I'm sure that, among other things,
we'll be talking about golf.

Two Guys Talking at the Four Horsemen Tavern

I was sitting at the bar alongside the
usual suspects, with their half-filled
ash trays and half-emptied glasses of
beer, when an old man seated in the
corner began toasting some Irish
whiskey with his friend.

And though their conversation was muffled
by the normal weekday chatter, I heard
what I thought to be a Gaelic verse, with
bits and pieces, throughout their discourse,
of aberrant phrases and colorful words.

So as the minutes went by
I continued to listen, for the occasional "shenanigans,"
or "donnybrook," or "shillelagh," but then the room
fell quiet and as clear as a bell
I could hear that old man's lilt distinctly say,

"He knew my face, he said I looked familiar,
like someone he used to know." Then a few
moments passed before the other man simply
asked, "Has he lost a lot of weight?"
And his question seemed to hang there, like smoke,
as he sat patiently and waited for an answer, until
the old man finally said, "He doesn't even know
that he's sick; he still thinks he's at home."

Then they toasted again,
a broken promise, to
remain always young.

Walking Past the Jeep Plant

That familiar scent of autumn has returned,
to this gritty city, to these forgotten neighborhoods,
to this crumbling relic of World War II
and it lingers ...

across these empty parking lots,
with their scorched metal barrels and knee-high weeds,
and down these desolate alleyways and streets
like a "blue-collar" ghost.

So unmistakable, though so eerily non-descript,
disseminating perhaps from the factory dregs,
from those rusted-out hollows
along the interstate.

Perhaps those fire-eaten kilns
held one final puff, just one last vestige
to be erased,

or maybe it's the charred remains
from some old sports page
filled with touchdowns
and battles won,

rising like a childhood memory
amidst a pile of burning leaves.

Yet, as these atoms and molecules
are being whisked away, they of unknown origin
wafting through space,

I need only to breathe
for them to become a part of me, once again,
with a lone smokestack now towering in the distance
but still bearing the name,

OVERLAND.

Rules of Engagement

I began watching from my living room, simultaneously
at first, with a pick-up game of street football becoming
a more-welcomed substitute for the world news,
after having listened to, and finally grown tired of,
those same old caveats and pretenses of war.

So, gradually, the endless droning about China
and North Korea and Syria and Iran ... disappeared,
no longer mattered, and went fading into the background,
as I slowly ascertained the boundaries of something
that I could at least *try* to understand.

Empirically, anyway, with the quarterbacks and receivers
adhering as best they could to their precocious signals, several
unspoken or otherwise numerical—about when to swerve or not
between the shrubbery—in their self-contained unit of asphalt.
With driveway end zones and sidewalk out-of-bounds and the
momentary disruptions for passing traffic, which were spent,
of course, arguing over the rules, or the degree of reciprocity
for their most recent failure, with no one willing to take the blame
for a "slant-cut" mistaken for a "down-and-in"
and another pass play gone awry.

But they would dust themselves off and huddle-up
to try again, hoping this time to get it right,
and begin professing once more
before being proven to be either trusting or gullible
when smashing into the line,
as if faith can be somehow learned.

Nine Miles to Trenton

> *Everything is at stake.*
> —George Washington (1776)

Your only journal entry on that
Christmas Day, now preordained,
with the fate of unborn millions
depending upon God and your suicidal
plan. Knowing full well that come the
thirty-first, but for your gritty little
handful, they would not re-enlist, so
weary after suffering so many defeats

and the latest of pell-mell retreats
through New York and New Jersey and
then finally to safety on this western
bank of the Delaware.

Even you,
just one week
earlier
suggesting *the
game is pretty
near up*
when writing your brother and then your wife

discussing interior decoration
and what crops to be planted next season
and the breath-taking vistas at Mount Vernon

when divine intervention or the sheer
insanity of desperation took hold,
though really not a choice with so few
options, but still, with so very much to
lose, your last name having already been
mutinied, ripped to shreds, like so many
near-misses through your overcoat.

But now, standing stalwart in your resolution
and once more tempting fate, while leading
your soldiers through the freezing cold,
with their brutal exhaustion beyond comprehension
but for you, statuesque when crossing.

Tiger Stadium

Everything is the past,
for what is, is no more,
and the future is yet to be.

Everything seemed green back then and cold
to the little boy at his first football game
sitting next to his dad. Surrounded by,
and inundated with, the indelible smells
of cheap-ass cigar smoke and so many spilt beers
while watching the numbers change on the
gigantic black board above the bleachers,
showing all of the other scores, from all of the other games,
in all of the other cities. And he was in Detroit!
He was actually there, sitting next to his dad.
The Lions won that day and he was so alive,
and so in love, with everything.

Everything had turned blue by then as the young man
was sitting in the sun watching his umpteenth baseball
game surrounded by his childhood friend. Yes, this stadium
was his everything. It was as if he could take the whole
place into the palms of his hands, give it a good shake,
and make it fake snow. He knew every entrance,
he knew every exit, he knew every square inch,
he was in total control. That was until some years ago,
when they suddenly closed the doors—forever.

Everything was white there in his dream
where his stadium now laid in ruins; a painful reminder
of what used to be, barely recognizable, but he knew what
it was. There was a partial shell with some pillars and posts
that had somehow moved to Toledo and stood next to his
childhood home—and as he encircled the catacombs of the
tunnels and the sarcophagus of the right-field stands, at first,
he couldn't find his way in, and then, he couldn't find
his way out—and all he really knew for sure was that
the little boy was lost.

Moon River

*Hanging on my basement wall
is a small rectangular picture, enclosed
in a 9x15 inch wooden frame, a drawing
of a bald eagle holding in its beak a banner
with the words "America Forever—1918,"
perched on top of Old Glory. An heirloom,
passed down through four generations, lastly,
from my father to me. The glass encasing, at times,
captures my reflection as I'm walking by.*

If I had known it was going to be the only perfect day
that I would ever have, I would have committed more to
memory. But, unfortunately, I am not one of those who can
remember when three, tying a shoe or blowing out a candle.

Instead I was seven, perhaps even eight, in the front yard on
a beautiful Saturday morning, crisp and clear with our crab
apple tree ready to burst wide open. I was bouncing a rubber
ball off of the stoop, sometimes the front door, then over the
roof, and riding my bicycle down the driveway and then up
again, while my parents were busy with their spring cleaning.

And as my father was in the backyard washing the windows,
I went inside and it smelled like lemons where my mother had
whirled around from room to room romantically dusting to the
songs of Andy Williams. However, my most vivid memory of
that day is actually a single moment.

I was sitting on my bike at the bottom of the drive watching
my parents, both at the same time, *framed* in happiness:
My father through the breezeway in his white T-shirt and blue
jeans with the backdrop of the world's greenest grass, while
my mother at that very instant was captured singing through
the kitchen window, one of her all-time favorite songs.

About You

My mother gave me a poem to read
she'd found in the local obituaries
titled, "A Mother's Farewell."
Instructions really, about how not to grieve
and not ever having to be alone,
even when that day comes for her,
for she would always be there
to welcome us home.

My mother, once again, thinking of others,
preparing well in advance
as is always the case,
very much before-hand
to comfort us, even after she's gone.

But mother,
before there is such a poem written
about you, another one begins
and it goes something like this:
Some of the kindest words ever thought
or spoken, though not always heard,
so many times *from* you, about others.
But, my darling mother, who gives so much,
these beautiful thoughts are more times
about you, many times from others,
but so many more times
from me.

The Stud Finder

The other morning, I had a constructive conversation
with my wife.

She's a District Manager for a candle company
and one of her stores was in need of a small shelf.

But, the thing is, she wanted to build it herself.

So, we discussed hardware.

The topics were mainly nails, screws, and wall anchors.

However, we also took the time to touch upon
a few other subjects, which included
the subtleties of a screwdriver,
the essence of a hammer,
the magic of a level,
and, of course, the mysteries of sheet rock.

Furthermore, I felt obliged, or dare I say compelled,
to demonstrate the proper usage
of a stud finder.

I explained that wall studs are usually spaced
16 inches apart, and showed her how to locate one
by slowly dragging the device along the wall
until it beeps and flashes.

Then, for a moment, I pointed the stud finder at myself
and said, "Hey honey, this damned thing must be
broken—it keeps beeping at me."

She gave me a little smile.

And honestly, that's all
I was looking for.

What I Did Today

Dropped off a bag of clothes at Goodwill.

Picked up some chicken at Howard's Meats.

Trimmed a few bushes by the back deck.

Straightened out the Memorial Day bunting.

Took our dog for a walk around the block.

Stopped to admire a neighbor's garden—and wondered,
just how many shades of green there were?

Noticed a droplet of water on a leaf—thought it was the kind of thing
a poet might write about.

Turned on the TV.

Read a message (as it was scrolling across the bottom of the screen)
that Manuel Noriega had died.

Stared at an empty white boat that was lying on a beach
in Zanzibar, Tanzania.

Looked "Zanzibar" up on my phone—it was 13,000 kilometers away.

Grilled some teriyaki chicken for dinner.

Went for a drive in my Jeep.

Glanced at the touchscreen—it was 73 degrees at 7:30.

Lowered the windows to feel the breeze—then realized
that Sister Cathy Cesnik was right:

There's nothing too small to have meaning.

Wrote a poem.

Put-In-Bay, Ohio

Every time I enter that harbor on South Bass Island, and go
walking down those tiny streets, it reminds me of this toy town
on which my friends and I used to play with our matchbox cars
when we were children.

One that came in a carrying case and was occasionally tucked away
only to be reopened in the summer to our amazement and delight,
with "Pete's Filling Station" and "Frank's Hardware Store"
and so many other colorful buildings; like the "Roundhouse Bar,"
where my friends and I used to drink from red buckets and then wear
them on our heads; and "Frostys," where I performed my very first
beer slide; and the "Beer Barrel Saloon," home of the world's longest
bar; and "The Boathouse," where Pat Daley would play his guitar
and sing until the wee hours of the morning.

Only now, my wife and I usually rent a golf cart
to drive around and visit the *even more* historic sites,
like Perry's Memorial—named for Commodore Oliver Hazard Perry
for his heroic exploits during the War of 1812.

Although, sometimes, if we're feeling a little zany,
we'll stop at the "Winery" and have a glass of White Zinfandel,
or perhaps a nice Chablis, before boarding the 7pm running
of the "Jet Express" and heading for home.

Not like that time when I missed the last ferry
and had to spend all night with a hoot owl above my head,
while lying there by myself on a small wooden bench
in the old depot.

Parkersburg

To be honest, after exiting the highway
and pulling into a "Stop 'n Go" to refuel,
I began thinking to myself that it was thankfully
the only time we'd be there;

and that the man standing in line next to me,
holding a pack of Marlboro's and a bottle of orange soda,
was most likely named Phil,
judging by the grease beneath his fingernails
and the word "Phil" stitched in red on his denim shirt;

and that the nameless white cat across the street
lying on a window ledge in that patchwork neighborhood,
consisting mostly of particleboard and tar paper,
was probably the fattest feline that I had ever seen.

Though, for a moment, as I gazed in awe at the mountains
of West Virginia, I imagined what all that green would look like
in the fall—when millions of trees, with names of which
I have never been certain, are exploding with color.

Then we got back on the interstate
and traveled farther south.

Dempsey vs. Willard

The world heavyweight championship fight;
July 4, 1919, at Bay View Park in Toledo, Ohio.

In un-Godly heat, well over one hundred degrees,
with the sap from the makeshift split-rails oozing
causing many of the gents to lose their britches
and cover themselves with newspaper while wandering around
the hastily built eighty-thousand seat stadium, and

with the famous western lawman Bat Masterson collecting
guns and knives at the gate, while trying to avoid any shenanigans
like drunkards bathing in the barrels of lemonade
thus ruining the lot for the folks getting hotter but

with the fight ready to begin and with "The Manassa Mauler,"
like a ferocious cat, pouncing on the enormous Willard
from the opening bell and knocking him down seven times
before being carried off by a frenzied and jubilant mob
only to return in the nick of time

with the threat of disqualification, for the referee
having never "officially" surrendered the match
to the chagrin of Dempsey's manager
who wagered most of his life's savings
on a first-round knock-out, but

with the second and third just a formality
for the beaten and battered Willard,
his face now grotesquely disfigured,
and when finally unable to take anymore

with five missing teeth and a broken jaw
and several cracked ribs,
the vanquished giant
quietly boarded a train for home.

When I Came Back Dying

My notebook was open, the TV was on,
when a narrator (describing the death of Paul Cezanne)
said, *after painting one day, he came back dying,*
while an empty sheet was patiently waiting
for my unexpected verb, for the nouns to somehow
become a perfect symphony of words,
to come trudging in through that newly laid snow
with their tiny footprints searching for
the tilting branches of the trees, or
a cool clean northern breeze,
or someone kneeling beside a headstone,
as an anonymous voice continued to recognize
the beauty of an artist's work.

I realized then, that everything is words,
either said or unsaid, printed or otherwise written,
while still trudging along and searching
for that feeling of total satisfaction from within,
if only once, now conscious of one's own mortality
and hoping to stumble upon Jesus
in the happenstance of a poem.

But only later did I realize that it was actually
a premonition of me when I came back dying
to an incomplete sentence,
making just the slightest impression
on an underlying page.

Serendipity

There's something about
a summer night's breeze,
the gentle persuasion
of dancing winds
playing with daylight's final
shadowy silhouette,
fragrantly sweet
and sprinkled with magic
for which you long
to scoop-up
and run,
faraway.

A Parallel Universe

I was sitting in my Jeep,
enjoying a pleasant August evening,
while waiting for my wife to pick up a few groceries
at the supermarket,

and as I was thinking about the nice steak dinner
that we were going to have,
with Portobello mushrooms and Vidalia onions,
and watching the sun melt into the horizon
like a slab of butter, someone in a black Audi,
with moon-roof open and Rap music thumping,
pulled into the space next to mine
and began to light-up from behind his tinted windows
like the Little Dipper.

Then he pumped-up the volume to blast his heartfelt lyrics
deep into that yellow-lined continuum
that we humans refer to as a parking lot,
the way I might've in a different time
or if I'd come from another planet,
say Mars or Saturn,

or perhaps if I lived in another dimension,
where there were no such things as boundaries or etiquette
and was oblivious to everyone else, like him,

when singing his poems or reading his songs
and probing for other life forms,

who find such exploits to be beautiful
and totally understand.

Monday Morning

We have a routine.

My wife gets up around 5:30
and goes downstairs with Charlie,
our little black and white Maltese Shih Tzu,
to take him outside for a walk.
Then, with his tail wagging,
he scampers back up the stairs
to sit with me on the bed for a few minutes
while my wife takes a shower and gets ready for work.

That's usually how it goes.

But things were different this past Monday
when a bottle of red nail polish
fell out of the medicine cabinet
and broke in the sink:

"Oh my God," my wife exclaimed,
upon the sound of breaking glass,
and when I rushed to the bathroom
to see what was wrong, at first,
I thought I saw blood.

Though once I realized that it was only nail polish,
and that she hadn't been hurt,
I said, "It's ok babe,"
and told her not to worry.

However, she was still quite upset
about having made such a mess,
and was having some trouble catching her breath,
so I began to help her clean.

And, eventually, things got back to normal,
with the nail polish having been removed from the sink
and with that healthy blush color returning
to my wife's face;

but with the puppy now cocking his head
and whimpering from our bed
not appreciating the fact that, for a single moment,
I had left his side.

So, thinking that I was funny,
I said to our puppy in a playful voice
(and one loud enough for my wife to hear from her closet),

"Charlie, you remind me of Diane
when she and I were first dating."

And, without missing a beat, my wife retorted,

"Don't worry Charlie, you'll get over it—just give him
a few years and your tail will be wagging when he leaves."

"That was a good one honey," I said.

Then I turned on the shower.

Victoria

Third seat,
by the window,
behind Corey.

She sometimes gets her foot caught
in his desk—don't ask how.

She says the most darling things,
when the room is quiet,
out of the blue:

"I got my shoestrings caught in an escalator once."
"I'm going to be sixteen years old in eight months."
"I like butter."

Such a sweet child.

Reunion

Walking to school
some twenty-odd years late
for the bell.

The terrain was strangely familiar
resembling some foreign land once visited
with nameless markers
for the dead.

But I enjoyed the fact
that I could still dissect the maze,

that I could navigate its passage evenly
and without effort,

with every nook and cranny slowly becoming
my own again;

though the child-sized stairs now seemed unnatural
and barely negotiable,

when taken one
at a time.

Across the Street from the Funeral Home

Yellow lines crisscross the blacktop
where children like to play,

where the foul balls and home runs
are cursed and chased

as they continue to roll like marbles
on the sidewalk

against their young pursuers' wishes
and in spite of their thrown mitts

and where there is recent moisture
of sweat and spit

whenever cars are not parked there
for special occasion.

The Last Laugh

We were both wearing frowns
when leaving the house today,
you to walk the dog and me
to go to work

and I'm sure it only made matters worse
upon returning home to find
that I had once again
unplugged your curling iron

and had stolen five minutes
from your hurried early-morning schedule
that you wanted to save

for making lunches and taking the kids to school
and feeding the dog before finally
getting yourself ready for work,

having been up since 5:30,

and for that I'm sorry—and I promise to never again
unplug any of your do-dads

once I'm dead.

For when my cold, lifeless body is six feet under,
or my ashes have been scattered to God knows where,
I won't mind (as much)

and you can keep your curling iron plugged-in
for as long as you wish, perhaps propped-up
next to the clothes iron as if they were married
and pretend that they never disagree,

until the day they set the house on fire.

And when I'm gone,

you can light your candles and keep them aglow
even when you leave to run errands

to the grocery store or to a gift shop,
or maybe to a nail salon,
or a fancy luncheon,
or to wherever it is that widows go,

but when you finally return
to see your house ablaze
I hope at that very moment
you'll think of me
and smile.

Because then,
perhaps through wistful tears
when remembering our fiery love,
you'll be certain

that your dead husband's soul is looking down,
thankful that you're safe,

and somewhere just waiting to tell you
that he was right.

Artistic License

Even now,
though our daughter has since moved
far away, that same picture is hanging
in her upstairs room,
of a little girl looking back
forlornly toward the ocean,
with her sandy blonde hair still neatly folded
though being gently stirred
by a late-afternoon breeze.

With the day complete,
carrying a sea-horse beach pail now empty
except for her dreams of returning one day
to Betsy Cameron's white-border world,
where her waving summer dress
will remain forever in sharp contrast
to the bluish-gray skies,
infinitely cloudy and overcast
when inside of *There's Always Tomorrow*;

with the irony of the title making the beauty
more sweet, and the sadness
more profound.

Van Gogh

While browsing through some poetry
at a local book store,

without seeing my own,

upon dissecting the newer selections
and then grumbling,

finding most contemporary writing
to be gibberish,

I thought of him;

a tortured genius
whose work was known by only a few
before shooting himself,

or so it's alleged,
having never found the gun,

and dying at 37
with his final words,

"The sadness will last forever."

And I wondered
if he was right,

while reading row upon row
of incoherent sentences,

while subjecting myself
again and again

to the assorted ramblings
of hip-hoppers, acid-trippers,
and second-graders

now referring to themselves
as poets

in a world no longer
of Wordsworth or Longfellow.

And I wondered
if his severed ear

was indeed
a gift for Gauguin

and why I continue
to write poetry

when
the social standing
for a poet

is perhaps
one rung higher
than that of a starving artist,

the future Van Gogh,

the painter who dies penniless
a century before

one of his creations is sold
for 82.5 million.

Though, I've heard it said
that a person dies twice;

the second time being
when your name is mentioned
for the last time.

Advice from a Sinner

Although
it's been several years
since my last meaningful
altercation,

I think that there are still times in this world
when a person must fight
for what he believes.

So, if you happen to find yourself in a confrontation,
one in which Jesus would turn the other cheek,
here's what you should say:

"You know, I may be a lot of things,
but one thing that I am not,
is afraid of you."

And when you say it—mean it.

For the secret to winning that fight,
or to winning any fight,
is to not be afraid to lose;
to take a punch,
to throw a punch,
to look like a fool,
to bleed, or even
to one day die.

Because then, no matter what happens,
you've already won—as long as you remember to ask Jesus
for forgiveness.

How It Begins

I slowly walked into the kitchen
on a snowy New Year's Day with
my mind like a TV that had lost its signal
from too much frivolity the night before.

And while my wife was preparing a pot roast
I began searching for a bottle of aspirin,
as she kept going along in conversation
about the kids and the sauerkraut and the weather.

Then as a voice on the radio was saying to expect
anywhere from four to another eight inches,
my wife surprised me with a challenging question
about two pans that were sitting on the counter:

one was circular while the other was more oval
but both were black with little white speckles,
and she asked if I'd be able to choose the one
that used to belong to her grandmother.

Well, hoping to maintain whatever dignity I had left
after a night of beer and whiskey and champagne,
I lightly clanked the metallic sides with my fingers
before pointing to the one in the shape of a circle.

"Nope," she said, in a rather victorious tone,
"it's the other one."

So, not wanting to admit defeat,
nor realizing that neither pan was empty,
I picked up the "other one" for a further inspection
and drenched myself with water.

And I thought, *this is how it begins,*
as I stood dripping on the floor,
for at that moment I just somehow knew
that my best years were behind me.

It's when you suddenly realize that as each day passes
you'll regress a little more,
as you're standing in a puddle
in the middle of your kitchen
but thankful,
that it isn't urine.

It's when you're wearing
a wrinkled flannel shirt and gray sweat pants,
and your face has a stupid grin,
but when your wife, of course, thinks it's funny
and laughs like it's still
your honeymoon.

And then, you laugh too.

Having Never Been to Idaho

I was standing alone
on a January evening
with my trusty snow shovel in hand,

like the Marlboro Man
with my breath slowly rising
staring out over a vast Ohio plain;

and flushed with that feeling of accomplishment
with my mountains and valleys complete
I began thinking of the Antarctic and Sir Ernest Shackleton
and of those astronauts who walked on the moon;

and of distant power lines and changing cloud formations
and of my prostate cancer and Alan Shepard,
and I wondered how much longer I had to live
and what my wife was preparing for dinner;

and I thought about the state of Wyoming
and how I once dreamed of riding the fences,
then I looked up at those clouds
the way Steve McQueen did in *Papillion* and said,

"I'm still here you bastards."

The Writer

"So," the reporter continued, in a series of probing questions, "what is your mechanism?"

"My *mechanism*," he repeated gruffly, implying that he was not at all pleased with her choice of words.

"Well," he said, as he put down his glass of bourbon and then began tapping his index finger on the side of his head, "it starts here."

"And then," he added, as he leaned in a little closer and held his old, callused hands in front of the reporter's face, "it goes here."

Then, he abruptly turned in his chair and began smashing the keys on his typewriter while shouting, "And then—it goes here!"

"You see?"

"*This* is the mechanism!"

"And then," he said once more, as he pointed at the sheets of paper that were lying on the floor, "it goes here."

Then he picked up his glass
and took a drink.

Charlie the Dog

As I'm writing this, he's burrowing into a pile of clean laundry, our full-grown Malshi of only ten pounds.

And I'm thinking back to when he was a puppy, with his baby-face and long white beard, how we used to call him "Dziadzia-boo," with dziadzia (jah-jah) being the Polish word for grandpa.

But my wife still likes to call him "Yittles," which is simply the word little with a "y" as in, "my yittle puppy who I love so very much," the phrase that she repeats on a daily basis.

Which is rather odd because, as I recall, it was my wife who made the rest of us promise to not talk "baby talk" to our dog, like they do in "some" families, and to not constantly hold him and kiss him as if he were a child.

Because, he's not a child—right? He's a dog! He's only a dog.

And yet, here we are—with *everyone* hugging him and kissing him and calling him all sorts of names.

Let's see, there's "bubba" and "boo-boo" and "puppa dog,"

and there's "Charlie Boy" and "shoo-shoo" and "chooch,"

and Charles Rutherford—with Rutherford, of course, being his middle name—when he's in trouble for having done something wrong.

That's because, after we first got him, my wife made a list of "puppy" names, with Walter coming in second and with Rutherford taking third. But, at the time, it seemed to make sense; after all, even the website said that in the name Rutherford was, "something which separates genius from the very good."

Well, it's been five years now, so you can take it from me, Charles Rutherford is no genius—of that, I am quite certain. However, he does have an extremely good heart, and this family has a few issues.

Making Love

I made my sense of what you said, only later,
about making love, about finding the time,
when we're setting alarm clocks and making sandwiches,
when we're blowing our kisses instead of kissing good-bye.

But I say love is that bread on the table,
love is that weariness at the end of the day,
love is like a breath on a winter's window
when you know where you've been and where you should stay.

And tonight, as we lie in the darkness,
should we both fall asleep with empty arms,
through the fog of my dreams I'll keep searching
and desperately trying to make my way back home.

Because love is when you find that place where you belong
and love is then doing what must be done,
for love is more work than it is math or science
and isn't only measured after each setting sun.

So those with castles, my dear, may still have nothing,
and those *with* something, have something to lose,
and though we've yet to answer all of life's questions
please know—that I'm always making love with you.

Apocalypse

This is hard for me to admit.

But, yes.

When standing in line at the grocery store
I'll occasionally glance at the covers of those tabloid newspapers
and read their sensational headlines.

I do not, however, believe that the world
is going to end.

At least, not anytime soon.

And it's not that I don't understand
the opposing point of view, especially when living
in such strange and scary times
of economic upheaval,
of war and insurrection,
of lawlessness and strife,
of dogs and cats living together
and so on.

But, no.

I do not believe that the world is going to end
now that the Mayan calendar is a thing of the past,
along with Y2K and Global Warming,
and the Cuban Missile Crisis and the "new" Coca-Cola,
and Hitler and Bin Laden and Disco.

And my hope in writing this
is that we can all breathe a little easier,
knowing that we still have time ...

to find Jimmy Hoffa and maybe Sasquatch,
and the Loch Ness Monster and Noah's Ark,
and perhaps even the true identity
of Jack "the Ripper."

Myrtle Beach

We walked down to the shore
on that cold April morning
clad in only sweatpants and hooded jackets,

and with some hardier souls
we formed a makeshift line
of plaid shorts, cut-offs, and sandals.

However, I didn't walk down to the shore
on that winter-like day
to see the sun lift itself and shimmer
upon the ocean,

as much as I walked down to the shore that day
to see my wife's face
when she's happy.

To see that sparkle in her eyes
when those glistening dark pools
shine like three-quarter moons,

and when through those eyes
the world becomes new

and everything about us
seems possible;

like a first kiss,

like a second chance,

like we're right where we belong,

with a tiny starfish lying in our path
as if showing us the way
to go home.

When the wind
and the sun
and the ocean
and the moon

are reminding me
of only her,

as we walked back to our hotel
across an old wooden bridge
just the two of us,
holding hands.

And in our room,
the scent of the ocean was upon us
and a glint of the sun's fire was still burning
in her eyes.

The Other Man

My wife likes Santa Claus.

In fact, at last count,
during this past holiday season,
there were approximately thirty-six
dolls, figurines, and cookie jars
decorating the inside of our house
with the old man's likeness.

However, though most are typically
red and round, what I found to be surprising was that
there are several others with different shapes,
colors, and sizes.

For instance, there's a couple in green robes,
and a few that are slender, and one (about three feet tall
and dressed in rags) who stares at me from the landing
whenever I open the basement door—he kind of creeps me out.

But, for the most part, they're all pretty friendly.

And that's why my wife likes him so much,
because he's decent.

Because he's a "good guy."

And that's why I've been thinking about
growing a beard and packing on a few pounds.

Maybe I'll quit working out.

And I'm thinking about smiling more,
and being nice to people,
and laughing.

Heck, maybe I'll even be kind.

After all, two can play that game.

Petoskey

It's our secret.

Kismet perhaps,
since we discovered it by accident,
when we became disenchanted
with the more popular and populated
Traverse City,

where we finally grew tired
of waiting in line and sitting in traffic
when simply wanting to have dinner
or perhaps look out upon
Grand Traverse Bay.

And at some point,
it became too much
and I wanted to leave.

But, I couldn't.

Because I didn't want to ruin it for her,
as I had done so many times in the past
by voicing my opinion at precisely the wrong time,
on birthdays and holidays
and other vacations,
so I thought,

No sir, not this time,

and for once
I kept my big mouth shut.

And God must have been pleased
because shortly thereafter,
through what can only be described as a miracle,
my wife wanted to leave as well.

Then we drove farther north
to wherever the wind might take us
and went twisting and turning along the shores
of Lake Michigan,

until we happened upon this quaint little city
sitting upon Little Traverse Bay,
an infamous hide-away of Hemingway's
that has become one of ours as well.

And though we're still planning
to remain at our current address
for a few more years,
my wife and I are now counting the days
to when we can take a deep breath
and go no further,

and finally share our secret
with each other.

Hope

It's one a.m.
and once again Charlie,
our little black and white dog,
is lying next to me on the bed
as we wait for my wife to drive home
from Frankenmuth.

He's on his favorite blanket,
the one with a plaid design,
mostly red and blue but interwoven
with the black and white colors
that he blends into and that used to be mine
when I was a child and under which
I would dream.

And still, even though
that bundle of tattered wool
now goes traveling around the house
to all of Charlie's favorite spots
for his morning and afternoon naps,

it's when he's back on our bed
and that old blanket is evenly spread
that he looks like a postage stamp,
lying so peaceful and quiet.

But then, his ears perk
and he sits up, thinking that my wife
has come home

(when he confuses the faint sound of the sump pump,
coming from the basement two stories below,
for that of the garage door opening)

and his eyes come alive,

and his tail begins to wag,
and he snorts and sneezes and becomes frisky.

But only
for a few seconds,
until there are no more sounds,

when he comes to the sad realization,
like me, that she is not here,

and he lays himself
back down.

And then, once again,
we wait.

Faith

The house is quiet.

I turned off the TV.

The weatherman said he was sorry for it being wet
and only 43 degrees—and I couldn't take his insincerity.

He reminded me too much of my doctor.

So I'm sitting here in silence
on this drizzly April day
with my dog wrapped in his blanket
lying next to me on the couch,
and with both of us still damp
from our early-morning walk.

But apologies aren't necessary—quite the contrary.

The honesty of the wind and the rain
was refreshing.

Though now, everything is quiet.

Our neighborhood is still.

Only the few hopeful notes of a robin
coming from just outside the window,
perched somewhere amongst the pink blossoms
of our plum tree.

And I was thinking, after months of recuperation
following my surgery, and on this tenth day
of my thirty-seven rounds of radiation treatments,

that I might be able to hang in there,
and land a lucky punch,
and win.

But, probably not.

And though I haven't as yet been able
to find the meaning of life, or sail around the world,
or climb to the top of Mount Everest—it's ok.

I appreciate God's candor.

The Grotto

On Monday, I poured some concrete.

On Tuesday, I prepared a stew.

I've been trying, you see, to find the right ingredients
for making life more beautiful, full of promise and hope,
like the statue of the Virgin Mary in our backyard
when her pink and blue pastels are surrounded by flowers
in the month of May.

Thus, on Wednesday, I went to have lunch at a delicatessen
in my old neighborhood, which is now full of rundown houses
and empty gardens, but where I overheard three rather interesting
words that I jotted down in my notebook to use in a poem:

innuendo, heebie-jeebies, and *periphery.*

Later, however, when I tried to add them to the mix,
like Monday's sand and gravel, or like Tuesday's carrots and peas,
they just stood there, like sinners outside of a church, or like peasant
children in Paris with their noses pressed against the glass
of a pastry shoppe.

Or like me in New York City
when standing in front of Bergdorfs or Tiffany's,
or when walking past Sax Fifth Avenue in Chicago,

or when sitting in front of my keyboard
and trying to write yet another verse
about my hometown of Toledo,

where I now feel anxious and nervous for whatever reason
and more like a foreigner every time I visit,

and to which I can no longer go about
building a shrine.

Delaney

My step-daughter is afraid of horses
and guys who dress-up like Santa Claus
and clowns

and no matter what I try to tell her,
whatever wisdom I may wish to impart,
her response is always the same—"I know."

Did I happen to mention that my step-daughter
is a teenager?

Once, a few years back,

after watching *The Blair Witch Project*,
I made scratching sounds on the walls of her bedroom
(which I later denied doing, of course,)
and it frightened her to the point

where

she went into her younger brother's room to sleep
which had to be like death to her

though death is something of which
she and others of her ilk
are apparently less afraid, at least

for now.

So, I'm not planning to share my thoughts with her
on the subject of dying. Not one word.

And I think it's ok if she's always afraid
of clowns.

The Polish Cavalry

During seventh grade history,
Sister Agnes Marie told us a story
about the Polish Army in World War II
and how they attacked the German tanks
using only horses and swords.

My classmates laughed.

"Boy, were they stupid," everyone said.

But not me. I thought they were brave.

In fact, I thought it was one of the greatest stories
that I had ever heard.

Though, who's to say?

Maybe there's a fine line between bravery and stupidity
depending on which side of history
you happen to be standing—
the victorious or the vanquished.

Then again, maybe my classmates were too young to realize
that one day, everyone must perish;

even the soldiers from the German 76th Panzer Division;

even the students from Saint Catherine's Grade School.

Even Shakespeare, who once wrote,

A coward dies a thousand times
but the valiant taste of death but once;

and Dylan Thomas, who later opined,

Do not go gentle into that good night.

So, I guess it comes down to one question
that we all must answer—sooner or later:

When the Grim Reaper knocks on your door,
and John Donne's bell begins to toll,
would you rather go out charging on horseback
versus a Nazi tank—with a sword clenched
in your bloody fist and screaming
at the top of your lungs—or while sobbing
into your pillow?

It's up to you.

Note: There've been a few reports in recent years
debunking this story as a fable, as a wartime myth;
however, some things in your heart you just know
to be true.

Bright Lights

My wife went to New York City last week
to give a presentation to her bosses.

She left from Detroit Metro on a Tuesday
and wasn't flying back until the weekend.

She visited Rockefeller Plaza and the Empire State Building.

And she said that the 9/11 Memorial and Museum
was incredible.

She hadn't expected to cry—but she did.

And after numerous meetings throughout the week,
her big speech was set for Friday morning at 10.
I remember looking at the time, on that day,
and saying a prayer.

Then she had lunch at Katz's Delicatessen
and her taxicab driver told her that in the past
he'd given rides to Mickey Mantle, Bernhard Goetz,
and Donald Trump—before "The Donald"
became president.

She'd even been staying in the same hotel
where Joe DiMaggio and Marilyn Monroe had lived
when they were married.

And while she was there, shining like a star,
I gazed each night into that easternmost sky that I knew
we still shared, and was trying my very best
not to miss her.

January

Sometimes,
amidst the silence,
on overcast days
such as this,

when alone,
in the emptiness,
by an old dirt road
or open field,

with infinite branches
in the morning sky
and new-fallen snow
on the ground,

my soul will yearn,
like a white-tailed deer,
to go into the woods
and disappear.

Heaven

Each morning,
my dog lies on my bed and waits
while I take a shower.

He watches the bathroom door. He stares at it.

I know this
because I leave the door slightly open
and can see him through the thinnest of cracks.

He's a good dog.

He's a patient dog.

His eyes are fixed. His gaze is set. He doesn't blink.

Then, when I've finished with my shower
and I'm drying off, I check on him
to see—and there he is,
still watching.

And, however odd it may seem,
this is how steadfast I imagine God to be
as he watches over each of us,

not to catch us in a wrongful act
necessarily, but rather to see the righteousness
with which we live.

So then, when the door opens and we are finally reunited,
my dog acts as if nothing in this world
could be as joyous.

That's how it must be.

Acknowledgments

I would like to thank Finishing Line Press and Shadows Ink Publications for publishing the following chapbooks in which the poems that are listed first appeared, sometimes in different forms:

Ode to Toledo (Finishing Line Press: 2006)

"Irene"
"Victoria"
"Reunion"
"Across the Street from the Funeral Home"
"Serendipity"

Two Guys Talking at the Four Horsemen (Shadows Ink Publications: 2007)

"Tiger Stadium"
"Something Genuine"
"Two Guys Talking at the Four Horsemen Tavern"
"Rules of Engagement"
"Walking Past the Jeep Plant"
"Talking About Golf"
"About You"
"Moon River"
"Artistic License"
"When I Came Back Dying"

The Hotel Victory (Shadows Ink Publications: 2009)

"Nine Miles to Trenton"
"Dempsey vs. Willard"
"The Disciple"
"Having Never Been to Idaho"

Daryl J. Lukas is the author of three chapbooks, a children's book, and a novel. He's a retired history teacher living in Temperance, Michigan with his wife, Diane, and their dog, Charlie.

He has two step-children, Delaney and Alex, currently living in Wisconsin and Ohio, respectively.

He was born and raised in Toledo, Ohio and earned a Master of Education Degree from the University of Toledo. He then taught for 32 years in the Toledo Public School System.

Besides reading and writing, he enjoys playing golf, lifting weights, drinking beer, puttering around the house, traveling with his wife, taking naps with his dog, joking with his friends, listening to old-time country (or classic rock 'n' roll,) going to Put-In-Bay, Ohio in the summer and watching his Ohio State Buckeyes play football in the fall.

However, above everything else, he believes that Jesus Christ is his Lord and Savior and that he died for our sins.

As If Faith Can Be Somehow Learned is his second full-length collection of poetry.

www.ingramcontent.com/pod-product-compliance
Lightning Source LLC
Chambersburg PA
CBHW070550090426
42735CB00013B/3142